REMEMBERING
THE PROPHETS OF
GOD

Book Eight

Russell M. Nelson

ALSO BY FRANCIS M. GIBBONS

BIOGRAPHIES OF THE PRESIDENTS OF THE CHURCH

Joseph Smith: Martyr, Prophet of God
Brigham Young: Modern Moses, Prophet of God
John Taylor: Mormon Philosopher, Prophet of God
Wilford Woodruff: Wondrous Worker, Prophet of God
Lorenzo Snow: Spiritual Giant, Prophet of God
Joseph F. Smith: Patriarch, Preacher, Prophet of God
Heber J. Grant: Man of Steel, Prophet of God
George Albert Smith: Kind and Caring Christian, Prophet of God
David O. McKay: Apostle to the World, Prophet of God
Joseph Fielding Smith: Gospel Scholar, Prophet of God
Harold B. Lee: Man of Vision, Prophet of God
Spencer W. Kimball: Resolute Disciple, Prophet of God
Ezra Taft Benson: Statesman, Patriot, Prophet of God
Howard W. Hunter: Man of Thought & Independence, Prophet of God
Gordon B. Hinckley: Man of Eloquence, Prophet of God

ORAL HISTORIES

Joseph Fielding Smith (Remembering Seven Prophets Book 1)
Harold B. Lee (Remembering Seven Prophets Book 2)
Spencer W. Kimball (Remembering Seven Prophets Book 3)
Ezra Taft Benson (Remembering Seven Prophets Book 4)
Howard W. Hunter (Remembering Seven Prophets Book 5)
Gordon B. Hinckley (Remembering Seven Prophets Book 6)
Thomas S. Monson (Remembering Seven Prophets Book 7)

OTHER BOOKS

Dynamic Disciples: Prophets of God
The Expanding Church
On to the Pole: The Autobiography of Francis M. Gibbons
Jesus Christ: Our Savior and Redeemer

REMEMBERING
THE PROPHETS OF
GOD

Book Eight

Russell M. Nelson

Reminiscences of Francis M. Gibbons

Edited by Daniel Bay Gibbons

Sixteen Stones Press

HOLLADAY, UTAH

Book layout, typography, and cover design ©2018 by Julie G. Gibbons

Sixteen Stones Press
6289 Howey Drive
Holladay, UT 84121

Russell M. Nelson
(Remembering the Prophets of God, Book 8)
by Francis M. Gibbons

Paperback ISBN 978-1-942640-25-7
eBook ISBN 978-1-942640-26-4

TABLE OF CONTENTS

EDITOR'S NOTE

This book is a collection of personal reminiscences about the life of President Russell M. Nelson, the seventeenth President of The Church of Jesus Christ of Latter-day Saints, recorded by Francis M. Gibbons, who was closely associated with President Nelson for over sixty years of his life. This work, part of a larger series entitled *Remembering the Prophets of God*, is the fruit of more than eighty hours of interviews I conducted with Francis M. Gibbons, my late father, between September of 2001 and April of 2016.

Volumes one through seven of the series were published in 2014 and 2015, during my father's lifetime, under the title, *Remembering Seven Prophets*. These volumes are my father's personal reminiscences about seven Presidents of the Church—Presidents Joseph Fielding Smith, Harold B. Lee, Spencer W. Kimball, Ezra Taft Benson, Howard W. Hunter, Gordon B. Hinckley, and Thomas S. Monson—with whom he personally worked over a period of more than four decades as a General Authority and secretary to the First Presidency.

Following my return from Russia, where I served as a mission president from 2011 to 2014, I conducted a final series of interviews with my father regarding his life and service. In those interviews, given between July 2014 and April 2016, Dad spoke at great length about his sixty-year association with President Russell M. Nelson, dating back to the mid 1950's. Dad left instructions that should President Nelson one day become President of the Church, it was his desire that an eighth volume of his reminiscences be published about President Nelson. The publication of this book fulfills that commission given by my late father.

"A Plutarch to the Presidents of the Church"

At his death in July of 2016 at the age of ninety-five, Francis M. Gibbons was perhaps the greatest student of the lives of the Presidents of the Church in this dispensation. He had two unique qualifications to speak and write about the Prophets.

First, during the last forty-five years of his life, Francis M. Gibbons was a kind of "Plutarch to the Presidents of the Church." This unusual phrase has reference to Plutarch, the ancient Greek writer and historian, who became the most famous biographer in history, the "Father of Biography." Many years ago my father shared with my mother his special aspiration to become "a Plutarch to the Presidents of the Church, and through writing about their lives to write the history of the Church." If any man or woman deserves the title of "Plutarch to the Presidents of the Church," it is my father, Francis M. Gibbons. Beginning in the 1970's, he became the most prolific writer of biographies of the Presidents of the Church, writing a full-length biography of every Prophet from Joseph Smith through Gordon B. Hinckley. Dad's published biographies of the Prophets have been very popular, selling hundreds of thousands of copies. Thirteen of his presidential biographies have been included in Brigham Young University's list of "Sixty Significant Mormon Biographies." He truly became "a Plutarch to the Presidents of the Church."

"A Scribe to the Prophets"

Francis M. Gibbons had a second unique qualification to speak and write about the Prophets: he was a personal witness and observer of the character of the last eight Presidents of the Church: Presidents Joseph Fielding Smith, Harold B. Lee, Spencer W. Kimball, Ezra Taft Benson, Howard W. Hunter, Gordon B. Hinckley, Thomas S. Monson, and finally Russell M. Nelson. Dad knew each of these eight men personally and worked with them at Church headquarters.

While serving from 1970 to 1986 as the secretary to the First Presidency and later as a General Authority, *Emeritus* General Authority, and patriarch at large for the Church, Dad associated with them on a regular basis. He takes his place in a long line of "Scribes to the Prophets," together with Oliver Cowdery, William Clayton, Thomas Bullock, Joseph F. Smith, George Reynolds, William F. Gibbs, Joseph Anderson, F. Michael Watson, and Brook P. Hales.

"I am their witness"

When Francis M. Gibbons was sustained as a General Authority in April of 1986, after serving for many years as the faithful scribe for the Presidents of the Church, he said:

> The Church is led by prophets, seers, and revelators. I am their witness. I testify that they are honorable, upright, dedicated men of integrity committed to teaching the principles of the gospel, who strive with all of their might to prepare a people ready for the return of the head of the Church, Jesus Christ, at His second coming.

In the larger work, *Remembering the Prophets of God*, of which this book is part eight, my father shared many unique stories, anecdotes, insights, and testimonies about the lives of Presidents Smith, Lee, Kimball, Benson, Hunter, Hinckley, Monson, and Nelson, which are nowhere else available.

On behalf of my father's family, we offer *Russell M. Nelson* and *Remembering the Prophets of God* for the enlightenment and inspiration of members and investigators of the Church and as a tribute to the memory of the last eight Presidents of the Church featured in these pages. I love and honor these great men and add my witness to that of my father that they were and are Prophets of God!

Daniel Bay Gibbons
Trustee, Francis M. Gibbons Literary Trust

Chronology of the Life of President Russell M. Nelson

May 17, 1893

Edna Anderson (1893-1983), mother of President Russell M. Nelson, is born in Ephraim, Utah. Edna subsequently receives all of her schooling in Sanpete County and graduates from Snow College. After graduation she moves to Salt Lake City, where she works as the director of the music department at the Lafayette School and sings in the Tabernacle Choir.

January 11, 1897

Marion C. Nelson (1897-1990), father of President Russell M. Nelson, is born in Manti, Utah. Marion lives only three years in Sanpete County and then moves with his family to Salt Lake City, where he attends Hamilton Elementary, Bryant Junior High, and East High School, where he is the student body president. After his father's death in 1913, when Marion is only sixteen years old, he begins supporting his mother, working as a newspaper carrier and soon a writer and editor for the *Deseret News*. While working for the newspaper he attends the University of Utah. While covering a concert of the Tabernacle Choir for the *Deseret News*, he meets a young soprano soloist, Edna Anderson, who soon thereafter becomes his wife. In his later years, Marion C. Nelson leaves journalism and becomes the president and general manager of the L. S. Gillham Advertising Agency, one of the largest and most successful advertising and public relations firms in the state of Utah.

August 25, 1919
President Russell M. Nelson's parents, Marion C. Nelson and Edna Anderson, are married in a ceremony performed by Elias S. Woodruff, bishop of the Forest Dale Ward and the publisher of the *Deseret News*, where Marion is then employed. After their marriage, Marion and Edna establish a family residence at 761 Roosevelt Avenue in Salt Lake City.

April 23, 1920
President Russell M. Nelson's older sister, Marjory Edna Nelson, is born in Salt Lake City.

September 9, 1924

President Russell M. Nelson is born at the Holy Cross Hospital in Salt Lake City.

May 29, 1926

President Russell M. Nelson's younger sister, Enid Fay Nelson, is born in Salt Lake City.

July 10, 1926

President Russell M. Nelson's parents move with their family into a home at 1428 Michigan Avenue in Salt Lake City.

March 26, 1931

President Russell M. Nelson's brother, Robert Harold Nelson, is born in Salt Lake City. In 1931 the family moves to 974 South Thirteenth East in Salt Lake City. President Nelson will remain in the home on 1300 East until 1963.

1935

President Russell M. Nelson skips the fifth grade at Douglas Elementary School.

1941

President Russell M. Nelson graduates from East High School. During his high school career he was a member of the varsity football team.

November 30, 1940

President Russell M. Nelson is baptized a member of the Church at the age of sixteen, following the diligent teaching and invitation of a home teacher, Jonas Ryser. Also instrumental in his baptism was Bishop Sterling W. Sill, later a General Authority; Hoyt W. Brewster, the priests quorum adviser; and President Joseph Fielding Smith, then a member of the Quorum of the Twelve and a member of the Garden Park Ward.

1945

President Russell M. Nelson earns his B.A. Degree at the University of Utah.

August 31, 1945

President Nelson marries Dantzel White in the Salt Lake Temple.

1947

President Russell M. Nelson earns his M.D. Degree at the University of Utah.

1947-1955

President Russell M. Nelson pursues his higher education at the University of Minnesota and Harvard University and serves in the Army Medical Corps.

1947

President Russell M. Nelson pursues joint surgical training and postdoctoral studies at the University of Minnesota. While in Minnesota, he works on the research team responsible for developing the heart-lung machine that supports the first open-heart operation in 1951.

1950-1953

President Russell M. Nelson serves as a Captain in the Army Medical Corps during the Korean War, being stationed in Korea, Japan, and at Walter Reed Army Medical Center in Washington D.C.

1953

President Russell M. Nelson obtains additional surgical training at Harvard Medical School's Massachusetts General Hospital in Boston.

1954
President Russell M. Nelson is awarded a PhD degree from the University of Minnesota.

1955
President Russell M. Nelson returns with his family to Salt Lake City and accepts a faculty position at the University of Utah School of Medicine. There he constructs a heart-lung bypass machine and uses it to perform the first-ever open-heart surgery in the state of Utah.

March 1956
President Russell M. Nelson performs the first successful pediatric cardiac operation.

1960
President Russell M. Nelson performs one of the first-ever repairs of tricuspid valve regurgitation. His patient was an LDS patriarch.

November 11, 1963
President Russell M. Nelson and his wife Dantzel move with their family from 974 South

Thirteenth East into the home at 1347 Normandie Circle.

December 6, 1964

President Russell M. Nelson is sustained as president of the Bonneville Stake, succeeding Frank B. Bowers. President Nelson's counselors are Albert R. Bowen and Joseph B. Wirthlin. Elder Wirthlin will later be called as an Assistant to the Quorum of the Twelve and as a member of the Quorum of the Twelve.

1967 to 1974

President Russell M. Nelson is chair of the Division of Thoracic Surgery at LDS Hospital.

1967 to 1984

President Russell M. Nelson is director of the University of Utah Affiliated Hospital residency program in thoracic surgery.

1968

President Russell M. Nelson performs a series of aortic valve replacements, demonstrating exceptionally low perioperative mortality. Later President Nelson performs the same operation on future Church President Spencer W. Kimball, replacing his damaged aortic valve.

1970

President Russell M. Nelson is awarded the honorary degree of Doctor of Science from Brigham Young University.

1971

President Russell M. Nelson is sustained as Sunday School General Superintendent (the title soon thereafter changed to General Sunday School President). One of his counselors is Joseph B. Wirthlin. While serving as Sunday School General President, President Nelson attends a meeting where President Spencer W. Kimball urges those present to learn Chinese. Pursuant to this challenge, President Nelson begins the study of Mandarin Chinese and acquires elementary proficiency. He subsequently develops ties to the medical community in China and makes several trips there to train surgeons.

July 11, 1971

President Russell M. Nelson is released as president of the Bonneville Stake, and is succeeded by Francis M. Gibbons.

August 1971

President Russell M. Nelson attends a medical conference in the Soviet Union, accompanied by his wife, Dantzel.

August 27, 1971

President Russell M. Nelson attends an historic meeting in Manchester, England, with members of the First Presidency and Quorum of the Twelve. This is the first meeting of the First Presidency and Quorum of the Twelve held outside the United States since 1840, when a similar meeting was held in Manchester, England.

April 1972

President Russell M. Nelson performs open-heart surgery on future Church President Spencer W. Kimball.

February 6, 1977

President Russell M. Nelson ordains his aged father, Marion C. Nelson, as an elder in the Church. President Nelson's father had been inactive in the Church for many years previously.

March 26, 1977

President Russell M. Nelson's parents, Marion C. Nelson and Edna Anderson Nelson, are endowed in the Salt Lake Temple and are sealed to President Nelson and his siblings for time and all eternity.

December 1979

President Russell M. Nelson privately publishes his autobiography, *From Heart to Heart.* He gives inscribed copies to hundreds of friends and associates, including each of the General Authorities of the Church.

April 7, 1984

President Russell M. Nelson is sustained as a member of the Quorum of the Twelve Apostles during General Conference. President Dallin H. Oaks is sustained at the same time. Presidents Nelson and Oaks are called to fill vacancies created by the deaths of Elders LeGrand Richards and Mark E. Petersen.

April 12, 1984

President Russell M. Nelson is ordained an Apostle and set apart as a member of the Quorum of the Twelve by President Gordon B. Hinckley.

1985

President Russell M. Nelson performs a quadruple bypass surgery on Chinese opera performer, Fang Rongxiang. He becomes the first person ever made an honorary Professor of Shandong Medical College.

1985

President Russell M. Nelson is assigned as the Apostle to oversee the work of the Church in Eastern Europe. Soon thereafter, with Dennis B. Neuenschwander and Hans B. Ringger, he is involved in the first meetings between LDS Church leaders and government officials in the Soviet Union, Romania, and Bulgaria. He also directs the expansion of recognition efforts in Czechoslovakia, Hungary, and Poland. Between 1985 and 1990 he visits thirty-one different countries as he begins his apostolic ministry.

1987

President Russell M. Nelson's book *Motherhood* is published by Deseret Book.

1988

President Russell M. Nelson's book *The Power Within Us* is published by Deseret Book.

1989

President Russell M. Nelson is awarded the honorary degree of Doctor of Medical Science from Utah State University.

1993

President Russell M. Nelson's short book *Lessons From Mother Eve* is published by Deseret Book.

1994

President Russell M. Nelson is awarded the honorary degree of Doctor of Humane Letters from Snow College.

1995

President Russell M. Nelson's book *The Gateway We Call Death* is published by Deseret Book.

1995

President Russell M. Nelson visits Beijing, China, with Elder Neal A. Maxwell at the official invitation of Li Lanqing, the Vice Premier of China.

1998

President Russell M. Nelson's books *The Magnificence of Man* and *Perfection Pending* are published by Deseret Book.

August 2003

President Russell M. Nelson becomes the first LDS apostle to visit the Central Asian country of Kazakhstan. While there, he visits with government officials, is interviewed on national television, and dedicates the nation for the preaching of the gospel.

February 12, 2005

President Russell M. Nelson's first wife, Dantzel Nelson, dies unexpectedly at the Nelson home in Salt Lake City.

April 6, 2006

President Russell M. Nelson marries Wendy L. Watson in the Salt Lake Temple.

2009

President Russell M. Nelson's book *Hope in Our Hearts* is published by Deseret Book.

2007 to 2015

President Russell M. Nelson is a member of the Church Board of Trustees for Education.

2009

President Russell M. Nelson, along with his wife and others, is attacked while on a Church assignment in Mozambique.

2010

President Russell M. Nelson's book *Wise Men Still Adore Him* is published by Deseret Book.

August 2010

President Russell M. Nelson travels to Kiev, Ukraine, to attend the dedication of the first temple in Eastern Europe.

September 2010

President Russell M. Nelson travels through and pronounces blessings upon the countries of Croatia, Slovenia, Macedonia, Bosnia and Herzegovina, and Kosovo.

2011

President Russell M. Nelson organizes the Moscow Russia Stake, the first stake of the Church in Russia. President Nelson also visits Kenya.

2012

President Russell M. Nelson organizes the St. Petersburg Russia Stake.

July 3, 2015

President Russell M. Nelson becomes President of the Quorum of the Twelve Apostles following the death of President Boyd K. Packer.

July 15, 2015

President Russell M. Nelson is set apart as President of the Quorum of the Twelve by President Thomas S. Monson.

August 20-31, 2015

President Russell M. Nelson makes his first international trip as President of the Twelve, to Central America.

September 2015

President Russell M. Nelson dedicates the renovated Aaronic Priesthood Restoration Site in Pennsylvania.

January 2, 2018

President Russell M. Nelson becomes the senior Apostle upon the death of President Thomas S. Monson.

January 16, 2018

President Russell M. Nelson's ordination as the seventeenth President of The Church of Jesus Christ of Latter-day Saints is announced at a live news conference in Salt Lake City.

"SIXTY YEARS OF CLOSE ASSOCIATION"

My acquaintance with President Russell M. Nelson and his family dates back to the mid 1950's. In 1954 my wife, Helen Bay Gibbons, and I purchased a home at 1784 Yale Avenue on Salt Lake City's east bench. We resided in the Yalecrest Ward in the Bonneville Stake. I soon became involved in the stake, being called as a member of the stake mission presidency and later as stake mission president.

In 1955 or so, a year after we moved into the stake, President Russell M. Nelson and his wife, Dantzel, returned to Salt Lake City after living many years in Minnesota and Boston, when President Nelson accepted a faculty position at the University of Utah School of Medicine. At the University, President Nelson constructed a heart-lung bypass machine and used it to perform the first-ever open-heart surgery in the state of Utah.

President Nelson also became deeply active in Church leadership in the Garden Park Ward and in the Bonneville Stake. For a time he served as a priests quorum adviser and then was called as a counselor in the stake YMMIA organization. In this setting I first became acquainted with him, as I was, at the same time, serving as a counselor in the stake mission presidency. My first impressions of President Nelson were that he was exceedingly young and brilliant. He was concise, punctual, and to the point in everything he did. I did not notice any unusual spirituality about him, however, and could never have guessed by his rather formal outward demeanor, the depth of compassion and innate spirituality that he would later develop.

In about 1958 or 1959 President Nelson was released from the stake YMMIA and was called as a counselor in the bishopric of the Garden Park Ward, under Bishop Hoyt W. Brewster. Bishop Brewster was an extraordinary man. He had previously served as President Nelson's priests quorum adviser in the Garden Park Ward. And Bishop Brewster had been influential, together with home teacher Jonas Ryser, in President Nelson's baptism at age sixteen.

The Garden Park Ward was a remarkable place to grow up, live, and serve for young Russell M. Nelson. It was a large ward of over a thousand members, and many prominent members and leaders of the Church resided there, including future Church President Joseph Fielding Smith, President Hugh B. Brown, Elder Richard L. Evans, and Elder Sterling W. Sill.

After his call to serve in the bishopric, I was often a stake visitor in the Garden Park Ward as stake mission president, and I continued to observe President Nelson's growth as a Church leader and administrator. He was an outstanding counselor to his bishop. It was remarkable, also, to observe how he created time to serve, notwithstanding his large family and his increasingly significant professional stature as a heart surgeon.

In 1964 my association with President Nelson entered a new phase, as we were both called to serve on the Bonneville Stake High Council, and then a few months later, when President Nelson was called as the stake president.

My later association with President Nelson included my service as his first stake executive secretary, my call from President Nelson to serve as a bishop, our close interaction during the years when he served as General Sunday

School President during the time I was secretary to the First Presidency, and then the years following his call to the Twelve in 1984. In the years after my release from active service in the Seventy, I served as a patriarch at large for the Church, and President Nelson had supervisory authority over this service as well. My final interaction with President Nelson occurred in August of 2015, when he attended the funeral of my late wife, Helen Bay Gibbons. Helen had served under President Nelson on the General Board of the Sunday School. On that occasion, President Nelson was so solicitous of the family, coming to the viewing and kneeling by my chair for a lengthy visit, preaching a marvelous sermon in tribute to my departed wife and companion, and then lingering after the service to go out of his way to shake the hands and speak with each member of my family, including my children, grandchildren and great-grandchildren! So, all told, my close interaction with President Russell M. Nelson spans from 1955 to 2015

Over the course of these sixty years of close association with President Russell M. Nelson, I have watched with great interest how he has grown and developed from a young convert to the Church and a brilliant doctor and surgeon, into one of the most remarkable Church leaders I have ever known. There was a unique quality about President Nelson, even as a young man. He radiated a calmness and a sense of great confidence. He was also one of the most naturally eloquent speakers I have ever known. When he spoke from the pulpit, he had the power to move the hearts of the people. He also was a superb delegator and had a gift for recognizing the innate talents of his fellow laborers in the Kingdom. For example, he had the foresight and genius to nominate Joseph B. Wirthlin as one of his counselors in the Bonneville Stake Presidency during his service from 1964 to 1971. Brother Wirthlin later served as an Assistant to the Twelve and as a member of the Quorum of the Twelve.

One of President Nelson's most salient personal qualities has been his capacity to grow and change over time. I have seen him grow in each of the six decades of our acquaintance. While he was a remarkable young man in his twenties and thirties, he has grown in his eighties and nineties into a truly wise, kind, Christlike, and spiritually sensitive servant of the Lord. At this juncture of time

[April of 2016], only the Lord knows what He has in mind for President Russell M. Nelson. However, I will say this. If he were to live long enough, in the providence of God, to succeed to the Presidency of The Church of Jesus Christ of Latter-day Saints, he possesses all of the qualities of a true Prophet of God.

"HIS FONDNESS FOR THE OLD NEIGHBORHOOD"

While serving as the president of the Bonneville Stake from 1964 to 1971, President Russell M. Nelson often spoke about his fondness for the tree-lined streets of the old neighborhood in Salt Lake City where he had grown up and where he spent most of his adult life. Except for the time he spent out of state during his military service and medical studies, this old neighborhood of the Bonneville Stake was his home from his earliest boyhood until his call to serve as a member of the Quorum of the Twelve.

When he was a young boy, his parents bought a home in the Yale Ward at 1428 Michigan Avenue. A few years later, the Marion and Edna Nelson family moved a few blocks west to 974 South Thirteenth East. In those days Thirteenth East was a very quiet, residential street, not the busy thoroughfare familiar to current residents of Salt Lake City. This last home was located in the Garden Park Ward, where President Nelson and his siblings, Marjory, Enid, and Bob, then grew up. The home was just up the hill from the beautiful Garden Park Ward building located on Red Butte Creek and was also within walking distance of Douglas Elementary School, and of East High School, where President Nelson later attended.

After his marriage to Dantzel, President and Sister Nelson lived in Russell's boyhood home on Thirteenth East, and in about 1963 or so, soon before his call as stake president, they moved to 1347 Normandie Circle. This final home of the Nelson family was located in the Yale Ward.

I believe that President Nelson's neighborhood in the Bonneville Stake was unique in three respects:

First, Bonneville Stake was located in a choice residential area. The homes in the stake were not expensive, large, or ostentatious. But it was a quiet and peaceful refuge and a wonderful place to live and raise a family. A rich variety of shade trees lined the streets. Most residents maintained flower gardens and well manicured lawns. The Church buildings located in the stake were focal points for family and neighborhood activity. The Bonneville Stake meetinghouse was in a beautiful setting in the heavily wooded gully of Red Butte Creek. Other chapels in the stake included the Garden Park Ward with beautiful gardens surrounding a quiet pool, the Yale Ward chapel located on Gilmer Drive, the Yalecrest Ward chapel located on Eighteenth East, and the Monument Park Ward chapel located on Twentieth East.

Second, the stake's proximity to the University of Utah gave it a kind of progressive, academic, literary air. The neighborhood was so close to the university campus that on Saturdays in the fall we could literally hear the roar of the crowds in the football stadium as we worked in our yards. The very names of the streets—Harvard, Yale, Princeton, and Michigan—had been chosen to lend the neighborhood some kind of homage to the gifts of learning and the power of education. The neighborhood was filled with professors, administrators, and employees from the University of Utah. For example, our neighbors both to the east and west of our home at 1784 Yale Avenue were owned by professors Dr. James Gibb of the Pharmacy Department and Dr. James King of the Geography Department.

Third, the neighborhood was convenient to the headquarters of the Church in downtown

Salt Lake City, and therefore was a desirable place for leaders of the Church to live. Over time the neighborhood was the home of Church Presidents George Albert Smith, Joseph Fielding Smith, Harold B. Lee, Spencer W. Kimball and Ezra Taft Benson; counselors in the First Presidency Hugh B. Brown, Alvin R. Dyer, N. Eldon Tanner, and Marion G. Romney; members of the Quorum of the Twelve Mark E. Petersen, Delbert L. Stapley, LeGrand Richards, Adam S. Bennion, Richard L. Evans, Joseph B. Wirthlin, Neal A. Maxwell, and Dallin H. Oaks; and many, many other General Authorities, including Sterling W. Sill, Henry D. Taylor, Theodore M. Burton, Joseph W. Anderson, O. Leslie Stone, Oscar A. Kirkham, Joseph L. Wirthlin, Thorpe B. Isaacson, Joe J. Christensen, Royden G. Derrick, and many others.

It is interesting to contemplate the impact that this neighborhood might have had upon the upbringing and developing discipleship of President Russell M. Nelson. First, it confirmed and enhanced his already strong feelings for the most important institution on earth—the family. It was above all a family neighborhood, and Russell and Dantzel Nelson's beautiful family of nine daughters and a son are near perfect exemplars of that ideal. Second, it was a neighborhood where young Russell was inspired by those around him to academic excellence and achievement. He was fired with ambition to succeed as a student, doctor, surgeon, administrator, and teacher. And third, he was brought into contact from his earliest years with Prophets and Apostles, who drew him inexorably toward a higher life calling as a disciple of Jesus Christ.

"His lack of Church activity as a boy"

In his public sermons as stake president and in private conversation, President Russell M. Nelson often reminisced about his lack of Church activity as a boy growing up in the Garden Park Ward. His parents were mostly less active in the Church during his boyhood. As President Nelson told it, his parents encouraged him to attend Church services, but almost never went with him. They would make sure that he put on his Sunday best and sent him out the door each Sabbath morning, but did not go with him. President Nelson confessed that he often diverted his path from home to the Garden Park Ward chapel to nearby Harvard Park, located at the corner of Harvard Avenue and Thirteenth East. There, he said, he and his friends would play football, while carefully watching the time. When the hour came for the conclusion of the meetings down the hill in the ward building, young Russell and his friends would return to their homes. President Nelson said that he often wondered why his mother didn't ask why he came home from "Church" each week so dirty and sweaty!

Because of his scanty attendance at Church and the indifferent attitude of his parents, President Nelson was never baptized as an eight-year-old boy, nor given the Aaronic priesthood offices of deacon, teacher, and priest at the customary years of twelve, fourteen, and sixteen.

By the time he was sixteen years old, President Nelson was a brilliant and focused young student at East High School, with a promising career ahead of him in any number of endeavors. He already aspired to become a doctor. But he was not a member of the Church, nor did he attend or express any interest in the doctrine or teachings. To a casual observer at that point in his career, his future as a Church member was, for all intents and purposes, a lost cause. But President Nelson was not a lost cause in the eyes of the Lord, nor in the eyes of his wise and caring priesthood leaders in the Garden Park Ward and in the Bonneville Stake.

"THE MINISTRY OF A FAITHFUL HOME TEACHER"

The ministry of a faithful home teacher in the Garden Park Ward, with the help of others, changed President Russell M. Nelson's life forever.

On several occasions I heard President Nelson relate with great emotion the circumstances surrounding his baptism. This surely stands as one of the hinge moments of his life and involves a home teacher, Brother Jonas Ryser; a priests quorum advisor, Hoyt W. Brewster; and a bishop, Sterling W. Sill. Also instrumental was President Joseph Fielding Smith, then a member of the Twelve, who lived in the Garden Park Ward and took an unusual interest in this brilliant young man in the neighborhood.

President Nelson was raised in a largely less active family in the Garden Park Ward of the Salt Lake Bonneville Stake. His father, Marion Nelson, was a brilliant man, talented, sociable, urbane, and successful. He was the owner and principal manager of the Gillham Advertising Agency, the largest advertising and public relations group in Utah, and had connections to most of the business and civic leaders of the city.

Brother Jonas T. Ryser was a high priest in the Garden Park Ward. As I recall, Brother Ryser and his wife, Thelma, lived in a modest house located on the west side of Thirteenth East. They were thus close neighbors with Marion and Edna Nelson, President Nelson's parents. Brother Ryser was a businessman, working for the Bailey Feed Company, and so had some business acquaintance with the advertising executive, Marion Nelson. Given this connection, Bishop Sterling W. Sill of the Garden Park Ward assigned Brother Ryser to attempt to make some inroads into the family as their home teacher. Initially, there was no progress made in softening the heart of the head of the household, but Brother Ryser persevered, visiting faithfully each month and forming friendships with the family.

At the time, young Russell was sixteen years old, and largely through the instrumentality of this faithful home teacher, Brother Jonas Ryser, and priests quorum adviser, Hoyt W. Brewster, he began attending the Garden Park Ward and was ultimately baptized a member of the Church.

I recall that in the late 1960's, while President Nelson was serving as the stake president in the Bonneville Stake, he called upon Brother Ryser to offer the benediction in stake conference, first giving a touching tribute to Brother Ryser, commenting upon the instrumental role this faithful home teacher had played in his own conversion. At the time, Brother Ryser was in his mid eighties, and as he made his way slowly to the stand, there was not a dry eye in the congregation. As Brother Ryser hesitated on the steps leading up to the stand, President Nelson stepped forward to assist him to the pulpit. It was a tender and electrifying moment for those of us who knew the history between these two men!

I attended the funeral of this Brother Ryser in the early 1970's, sitting by President Nelson on the stand, and marveled at the significant impact a faithful, humble home teacher can make in the lives of those he teaches, and upon the Church. During the funeral of Brother Ryser, President Nelson leaned over to me and whispered with some emotion, "This man changed the course of my entire life!"

Jonas Ryser typifies the kind of dedication we would like to see in all of the home teachers of the Church.

"NINE LOVELY DAUGHTERS"

Dantzel Nelson, President Nelson's first wife, was every bit as remarkable as her more famous husband. She was strikingly beautiful, wise, loving, sociable, and musically gifted to a very high degree. Dantzel mothered ten children with President Nelson, including nine beautiful daughters, followed by one son of great promise. For the entire time of his service as president of the Bonneville Stake, however, the Nelsons had nine children—nine lovely daughters—as the son was born after his release in 1971. So it was really something for the members of our stake to be presided over by this amazing family founded by young Russell and Dantzel Nelson.

The nine Nelson daughters and their mother often performed and sang together in the Bonneville Stake and created quite a sensation. As I recall, they played a variety of instruments, including violin, viola, cello, flute, and harp. They also sang beautifully. They were often called upon to sing in Church meetings in the Yale Ward or in the Bonneville Stake. The girls were also physically beautiful and turned many a head of young men in the stake and neighborhood.

President Gordon B. Hinckley shared an insight with me about President and Sister Nelson's daughters. President Nelson was close to both President Hinckley and the late President Stephen L. Richards, who was a member of the Twelve and later a counselor in the First Presidency under President David O. McKay.

President Hinckley told me that President Nelson was offered a prestigious scholarship at the University of Chicago. By that time President Nelson and Dantzel had several little girls. They were obviously concerned about the ramifications of moving their family to Chicago. President Nelson was personally acquainted with President Richards of the First Presidency. Accordingly, as Russell and Dantzel were deciding whether to accept the offer at Chicago, he made an appointment to go in and visit with President Richards. In the interview Russell laid out the opportunity that had been presented to him and asked for President Richards' advice. President Richards merely looked at Russell over his glasses and asked, "All of those little daughters living in Chicago?"

That was his way of indicating that it sounded like a bad idea.

President and Sister Nelson never accepted the scholarship.

"A BLUE BABY BLANKET"

The birth of the Nelson's only son, Russell M. Nelson, Jr., was a noteworthy event in the memory of members of the Bonneville Stake. There was quite an age gap between the youngest Nelson daughter and this final, tenth child, and of course there was much speculation "on the street" about whether Dantzel Nelson would bear a tenth daughter, or perhaps a son.

The Nelsons lived in a lovely home on Normandie Circle. There was a flagpole in front of their house. I recall that upon the birth of Russell and Dantzel's youngest child and only son, Russell M. Nelson, Jr., one of their neighbors, upon hearing the joyous news, ran outside with a blue baby blanket and ran it up the flagpole, thus announcing to all of the neighbors and ward and stake members that our beloved Dantzel and Russell Nelson finally had a son!

Russell Jr. grew up in the neighborhood with auspicious promise surrounding him from his birth. He was mentioned by name in General Conference on the occasion of his father's call to the Twelve. And he became one of the first missionaries ever to be called to serve in Russia. While in Russia, he translated for his father, who was perhaps the key figure in the opening of the former Soviet Union to the preaching of the gospel. Together with his older sisters, Russell M. Nelson, Jr. is a member of one of the most remarkable families in the Church.

"Under the tutelage of Bishop Brewster"

Aside from the impact of Brother Jonas Ryser, President Nelson's connection with the family of President Joseph Fielding Smith was equally impactful upon his early Church training.

Numerous members of President Joseph Fielding Smith's family resided in the Bonneville Stake, including his sons Joseph Fielding Smith, Jr. and Douglas Smith. Also, residing in the stake was President Smith's daughter, Naomi Smith Brewster, who was married to Hoyt W. Brewster, the priests quorum adviser in the Garden Park Ward.

Hoyt Brewster became almost a spiritual father to the young convert. At the time, President Nelson was concluding his schooling at East High School and beginning his university studies at the University of Utah. He was a brilliant student, and he advanced rapidly in his career path, beginning medical school at about age nineteen or twenty.

At the same time of his rapid progress in his medical training, however, Russell M.

Nelson was progressing rapidly in the spiritual realm under the leadership of Garden Park Ward Bishop Sterling W. Sill, and priests quorum adviser, Hoyt Brewster. The Bishop was giving young Russell a crash course in Church leadership and administration. President Nelson finished his bachelors and medical degrees in record time and left Salt Lake City to continue his education, receiving a PhD at the University of Minnesota and post-doctoral training at Harvard University.

By the time President Nelson had finished his education, Bishop Sill had been released as bishop and replaced by Hoyt Brewster. In 1955, President Nelson returned home to Salt Lake City for good, accepting a faculty position at the University of Utah and commencing a busy surgical practice. The Nelsons returned to the Garden Park Ward and picked up where they left off. In a surprising but inspired move, Bishop Brewster called young Russell, barely in his thirties, to serve as one of his counselors in the bishopric. This was in a day and age when the overwhelming majority of ward and stake priesthood leaders were in their fifties, sixties, or seventies. At the time, President Nelson was by far the youngest member of a bishopric in the stake.

It was while President Nelson was serving as a counselor in the stake YMMIA that I first met him. My interaction increased after his call as a counselor to Bishop Brewster. At the time, I was serving as the stake mission president, and frequently visited the Garden Park Ward. Even at his extremely young age, President Nelson displayed all of the hallmarks of his future ministry as an Apostle—he was exact and punctual in his habits, warm in his personal relationships, and eloquent in his speech. It was also evident that his tutelage under Bishop Brewster was bearing fruit. In Bishop Brewster he enjoyed the closest kind of interaction with a truly dedicated and able priesthood leader.

"RAPIDLY SCHOOLED IN CHURCH ADMINISTRATION"

After serving as the stake mission president in the Bonneville Stake, I was called in 1964 as a member of the stake high council. This was a unique and growth-inspiring experience for me, in large part because of the caliber of the men with whom I served. The high council met in a large room in the west annex of the Bonneville Stake center, seated in large leather arm chairs arranged in a semi circle facing a table behind which sat the stake presidency: President Frank B. Bowers and his counselors, Ira B. Sharp and Ferdinand E. Peterson.

As I said, I was the junior man in the august group. Next to me, in ascending order of seniority, sat Joseph B. Wirthlin, who had recently been released as a bishop of the Bonneville Ward. Next to Brother Wirthlin sat Russell M. Nelson, recently released as a counselor in the bishopric of the Garden Park Ward. At the time, Joseph and Russell were relatively young men, Russell still being in his thirties, and Joseph in his early forties. On the other end of the circle sat the senior high councilors, including Harold H. Bennett, who by that time had served on the Bonneville Stake high council for more than a quarter of a century, and Joseph Anderson, who had served for a similar period of time. Brother Anderson was the secretary to the First Presidency, having already served in that capacity for forty-two years, since early in the administration of President Heber J. Grant.

President Nelson's friendship and Church association with Joseph B. Wirthlin is an interesting one. They ultimately served together in four separate settings over a period of more than forty years. First, they served together, as I said, as junior members of that high council. Brother Wirthlin later served as President Nelson's counselor in the stake presidency throughout much of the 1960's. Later, beginning in 1971, they served together in the General Sunday School Presidency until Elder Wirthlin's call as a General Authority of the Church. And, more than a decade later, they began a long association as fellow members of the Council of the Twelve Apostles.

President Nelson's service on the high council was relatively brief, as within a few months of his call, he replaced President Frank B. Bowers as president of the Bonneville Stake.

It has since been an interesting thing to contemplate how President Nelson was so rapidly schooled in Church administration by such great men. Indeed, his priesthood schooling was as rapid and accelerated in many respects as his university and medical education. It is obvious that the Lord has had His eye upon this unusual servant of the Lord throughout his life and placed him in the circumstances He did so that he could be schooled spiritually to prepare him for what was ahead.

"I CAN'T GET THAT YOUNG DR. NELSON OUT OF MY MIND"

In late 1964, President Frank B. Bowers, president of the Bonneville Stake was released after nearly a decade of service.

The leadership of this single stake became a magnificent training ground for many future Church leaders for a period of more than half a century. President Bowers had been preceded in his calling as stake president by President Joseph L. Wirthlin (father of Joseph B. Wirthlin), later the Presiding Bishop of the Church; and by President Marion G. Romney, later an Apostle and member of the First Presidency. And President Bowers was succeeded as stake president by President Russell M. Nelson, future Apostle and President of the Church, who selected as a counselor Elder Joseph B. Wirthlin, later a member of the Twelve.

Elder Spencer W. Kimball, then one of the senior members of the Twelve, was assigned to effect the reorganization of the stake presidency, assisted by Elder LeGrand Richards, also of the Twelve. (Parenthetically, I should note that twenty years after the stake reorganization, Russell M. Nelson would be called to the Twelve to fill the vacancy created by the death of LeGrand Richards).

As part of the reorganization procedure, the two members of the Twelve interviewed all of the principal stake leaders and the bishops to obtain their nominations as to who should be called as the new stake president. At the time, I was a junior member of the high council, and so I was scheduled to be interviewed on Saturday morning, along with the other leaders.

On Friday evening, a reception, dinner, and social were held at the stake center to honor the visiting Apostles. Elder Kimball and Elder Richards attended with their wives. Also present were all of the members of the outgoing stake presidency, the high council, and the bishoprics, with their companions. It was a lovely affair. Tables were set up in the reception room, between the chapel and gymnasium. The decorations were lavish, carrying out the Christmas theme. I remember that there was a roaring fire in the fireplace in the reception room and a spirit of peace and serenity pervaded the entire evening. The two Apostles and their wives spoke briefly.

In his remarks before the roaring fire, President Kimball remarked that he brought with him an honorable release for President Frank Bowers, who had served a total of 36 years either as a bishop, member of the high council, or in the stake presidency of the Bonneville Stake.

The next morning, Saturday, December 5, 1964, at about 9:00, I was interviewed by the two Apostles. It was a heart-stopping event for me, to be in the presence of two such great men. They put me at ease, however, and treated me with great respect and kindness. My interview, like the others, lasted five minutes at most.

During my interview, which was conducted in the office of the stake president, the two Apostles sat on one side of the desk and I sat on the other. President Kimball was the senior Apostle, and so he conducted the interview and did most of the talking, while Elder Richards took notes. I was asked a few questions about my family and profession and about my testimony. Finally, I was asked to give the Brethren the names of three or four men who had the capacity to serve as a stake president. I recall that I recommended Joseph B. Wirthlin, Hoyt W. Brewster, Ferdinand E. Peterson, and T. C. Jacobsen. The Brethren were keeping a tabulation of recommendations made by the men being interviewed.

I also recall that during my interview, President Kimball asked me about my family and temporal situation in reference to the possibility of our filling a mission!

At the time, I suspected the two Apostles were applying methods used by the Prophet Joseph Smith in translating—namely, studying it out in their minds, pondering it in their hearts, and then seeking God in prayer for a confirmation or rejection of their conclusions.

That afternoon, Saturday, I attended a leadership meeting and was seated by Albert R. Bowen, who also served on the high council. Albert, who was several years older than me, was a practicing attorney and the son of the late Apostle, Elder Albert E. Bowen. I recall that during the meeting President Kimball entered the back of the chapel while a speaker was addressing the brethren from the pulpit, and sat quietly in a seat directly behind Albert and me. After a few minutes, President Kimball leaned forward and in his distinctive, whispery voice said, "Albert, will you please wait a few minutes after I leave and then join Elder Richards and me in the high council room?" After he said this, President Kimball slipped back out of the chapel. Albert was noticeably shaken and sat quietly without speaking for a few minutes and then left the chapel. I later learned that upstairs in the high council room, Albert was called as first counselor to President Russell M. Nelson.

The next day, Sunday, President Nelson and his counselors were sustained. At the same meeting, I was released as an alternate high councilor and sustained as a high councilor. Later, after the meeting, my family joined with the two Apostles, President Nelson and his counselors, Albert E. Bowen and Joseph B. Wirthlin, and their families in the high council room, where we were all set apart. Elder Richards set me apart.

That evening in my diary, I recorded, "This weekend has taught me, as few things have, that God, not men, dictates the selection of who serves in His kingdom. This new President has been called by revelation. May God bless and sustain him. May I, too, sustain and assist him with all my heart and energy!"

Several years later, after I began serving as secretary to the First Presidency, I heard the rest of the story of President Nelson's call from Elder Richards. For many decades it has been the custom of the First Presidency and the Quorum of the Twelve to have lunch together in a small dining room adjacent to the Upper Room of the Salt Lake Temple. This was a singular privilege for me, the Brethren's secretary, to join the fifteen men of the First Presidency and Twelve for this luncheon. One Thursday, the table conversation turned to President Russell M. Nelson, then serving as the General President of the Sunday School organization. Elder Richards said, in effect, "On Saturday, after we had completed all of our interviews of the leaders of the stake and prayed for guidance, President Kimball turned to me and said, "Well, LeGrand, how do you feel about it?' I answered, 'I just can't get that young Dr. Nelson out of my mind.' Spencer slapped his hand upon his knee and said, 'I feel the same way!' And that was the end of it."

"President Kimball was reading incomplete tithing records"

President Nelson shared with the high council this amusing anecdote regarding his call as stake president. During his private interview with the two visiting Apostles, Spencer W. Kimball and LeGrand Richards, President Kimball at one point asked President Nelson, "Are you a full tithe payer?" President Nelson responded, "Of course." President Kimball responded, in essence, "Well, all right, but I would have thought a doctor would be doing a little better financially."

President Nelson's mind was preoccupied by the unusual experience of being interviewed by two Apostles and did not fully comprehend what President Kimball was trying to say. However, later at home, as President Nelson ran over the interview again in his mind, the significance of what President Kimball was trying to say dawned on him. Obviously President Kimball was reading incomplete tithing records from the Nelsons' new home ward. The family had moved near the end of the prior calendar year from the Garden Park Ward to their new home on Normandie Circle in the Yale Ward.

President Nelson quickly checked his tithing records for the previous year and discovered to his horror that the tithing he had paid for eleven months In the Garden Park Ward had not been added to the tithing he had paid for only a single month in the Yale Ward!

President Nelson said that he was mortified by the discovery and wondered what the Brethren must think of him. This thought soon was replaced by other concerns, however, as he was soon thereafter summoned back to the Bonneville Stake Center, where the call was issued to him to serve as the new stake president.

"FELICITOUS CHOICES FOR HIS TWO COUNSELORS"

President Nelson selected Albert E. Bowen, son of a former Apostle, and Joseph B. Wirthlin, son of a former Presiding Bishop of the Church, as his counselors in the stake presidency. These were felicitous choices for his two counselors, as both men were superb administrators and as deeply steeped in Church doctrine and leadership as any two men in the Church could be. In these choices, President Nelson exhibited one of the wisest leadership moves a bishop or a stake president can make. As President Nelson often advised, a bishop should select counselors who are strong where he is weak.

There is no doubt that at the time of his selection as stake president, Russell M. Nelson lacked church leadership experience. He was still a very young man.

At the time of the President Nelson's calling as president of Bonneville Stake, the now-common office of stake executive secretary did not exist. However, several years later, under the principal advocacy of President N.

Eldon Tanner, this position was created church wide. President Tanner felt that an officer was needed to assist stake presidencies, attend all of the administrative meetings, prepare agendas, and follow up on assignments. When that position was created in 1969, I was called by President Nelson to serve as the first executive secretary in the Bonneville Stake.

In that new position, I began to attend all of the meetings of the Bonneville Stake presidency. My time serving as the stake executive secretary under President Nelson yielded a host of insights about President Nelson and his character.

President Nelson's choice of counselors was most interesting and illuminating. When he called me as a bishop in 1969, he told me that I ought to nominate "counselors who are strong where he is weak." He then added, "That is exactly what I have done."

Recognizing his lack of practical administrative experience, President Nelson nominated as counselors in the stake presidency two men with as deep a grounding in the Church as you could possibly find. Presidents Bowen and Wirthlin were two of the hardest working, wise, and Church-trained men in the Church. It was particularly important that President Nelson have such strong counselors, as his professional life made it difficult to devote the amount of time otherwise necessary to guide one of the largest stakes in the Church. During the administration of President Nelson, his worldwide reputation as a heart surgeon placed him in high demand, not only with performing delicate surgeries, but also in teaching, lecturing, traveling, and sitting on the boards of prestigious medical bodies. It was a great blessing for President Nelson to have two counselors, who, in President Nelson's own words, were "strong where he was weak."

It is fascinating the way that the lives of President Nelson and President Wirthlin were interwoven over several decades. They sat together, side by side, as junior members of the stake high council. Later they served together in the stake presidency. In 1971, they served together again as members of the General Sunday School Presidency, and following President Nelson's and Elder Wirthlin's calls to the apostleship in 1984 and 1986, respectively, they served together in the Quorum of the

61

Twelve for over two decades, until President Wirthlin's death.

"I DIDN'T WANT ANYONE TO STEP ON MY HANDS"

Elder Joseph B. Wirthlin was a fine football player as a boy, playing both at East High School and at the University of Utah. One day in stake presidency meeting in the Bonneville Stake, the subject of football came up, and mention was made of President Wirthlin's storied athletic career. President Nelson surprised us all by speaking up, saying, "I played football at East High School, as well." He then told this story: In high school he tried out for and made the team, but then began to have regrets. He was close to graduating from school and already had a scholarship offer to attend the University of Utah, where he had ambitions to become a doctor. Before the first game of his senior season, he went to the coach, Mickie Oswald (who was a member of the stake), and said he was concerned about getting his hands injured during a game. "I didn't want anyone to step on my hands in a pile-up," he said. Coach Oswald agreed that he shouldn't play, and so he kept him on the bench for the entire season.

There is an inspiring component to this amusing anecdote. Years later, President Nelson performed delicate heart surgery on his former coach, Mickie Oswald, and saved his life!

"A DREAM TO TRAVEL AROUND THE WORLD"

During the years I served under President Nelson in various callings in the Bonneville Stake, I was privileged to hear him relate several fascinating and illuminating details about his boyhood. One of these was shared in a meeting of the stake presidency while I served as stake executive secretary. President Nelson related the following experience.

While attending Douglas School, he was asked, together with all of the school children in Salt Lake City, to write down two lifetime ambitions. These goals were then collected and sealed up, and a monument was built on the west side of the City and County Building. President Nelson and his little schoolmates attended the dedication of the monument.

President Nelson said that he recalled that one of his ambitions, thus recorded, was a dream to travel around the world. President Nelson told us that he had recently fulfilled this dream, by traveling around the world with Sister Dantzel Nelson and a group of heart surgeons from the United States. The surgeons all participated in a medical forum in India. Since they would be traveling halfway around the world, they all decided that they would travel home the other way, thus completing a circumnavigation of the globe. The countries they visited included England, Russia, India, Thailand, Malaysia, and Japan.

Upon his return home from this trip in 1967, my wife and I were invited to President Nelson's home, where he and Dantzel showed us, a series of color slides they had taken on this lengthy trip.

The boyhood dream to "travel around the world" has taken on a far more serious and significant implication since President Nelson's calls, first as a General Church officer in 1971, and then as a member of the Quorum of the Twelve in 1984.

"Playing Bach on the Chapel Organ"

President Nelson had a fine singing voice, as do all of the members of his family. When he sang in meetings of the Bonneville Stake high council or stake presidency, it was evident that he had the finest natural voice in the room. This talent, of course, was inherited from his mother, Edna Anderson Nelson, who was a noted soloist with the Tabernacle Choir at the time his parents first met in the early 1920's. President Nelson's wife, Dantzel, also had a beautiful singing voice, and she also sang in the Tabernacle Choir for many years. This same talent was passed on to the next generation of Nelsons, and Russell's and Dantzel's nine daughters frequently sang together. President Spencer W. Kimball often mentioned the overwhelming spirit he felt when he first heard "those nine beautiful daughters" singing together during a stake conference visit to the Bonneville Stake.

One evening my wife, Helen, and I dined with President and Sister Nelson at the home of Albert and Margaret Bowen and gained further insight into President Nelson's musical sensibilities. President Nelson told us that one of his great grandfathers had been converted a member of the Church while he was a prisoner in jail. Two missionaries were also incarcerated at the same time, and the Nelson ancestor was impressed by their faith and humility, but especially by their singing in the jail! The music had more power to move the listener than even the Word!

One of President Nelson's initiatives as president of the Bonneville Stake was to foster and encourage the performance of first-rate music in Church meetings. There was a tradition of having a full orchestra, known as the Bonneville Strings, perform in many sessions of stake conference. Members of this large ensemble included musicians from the Utah Symphony or from the nearby University of Utah faculty.

Aside from hearing the President sing, however, I was unaware of his true musical talent, until early one Sunday morning, when I went to the building early to prepare for stake presidency meeting. Opening up the stake offices located on the west end of the stake center, I heard music coming from the chapel. I went down to investigate and saw President Nelson sitting at the organ console, playing Bach on the chapel organ! I sat down at the back of the darkened chapel and listened. I was astounded at his skill on the keyboard. When he was finished, he turned off the organ and walked to the back of the chapel, where he saw me. I complimented him on his playing, and he told me that he loved playing Bach and that it gave him great peace. He told me that he tried to play as often as he could, especially early in the morning. This opened my eyes to another unique quality of this most extraordinary man.

"THE FIRST SUCCESSFUL TRANSPLANT"

I recall that the news of the world's first successful heart transplant, which occurred in Cape Town, South Africa, in December of 1967 by Dr. Christian Barnard, created a tangible stir in the ranks of the members of the Bonneville Stake. At the time, President Russell M. Nelson was continuing his ministry as stake president. It was well known that President Nelson had been one of Dr. Barnard's classmates at the University of Minnesota, and that he also was a world pioneer in open-heart surgery. It was this event, without a doubt, which caused members of the stake, myself included, to look upon our young stake president in a new light. He was a truly remarkable man. President Nelson's rapid professional growth and establishment of an international reputation in his specialty only redounded to the glory of the Church.

"THIS NEWLY EMERGING SPIRITUALITY"

In his public sermons in the stake, President Nelson often enjoined the members not to counsel the Lord, but rather to seek and then do His will. It became something of a theme of his later service in the stake presidency. There was a growing spirituality in him that was very evident. His sermons were acquiring a spiritual power that was almost tangible. President Nelson's own life was a marvelous example of this attitude of seeking God's will and doing it.

And by doing God's will, Russell M. Nelson developed truly remarkable spiritual and leadership gifts.

The longer he served in the difficult and time-consuming role of stake president, the more he appeared to me to grow in stature and spirituality. It was like watching the process of a refiner's fire to observe him first hand. He started his service with a distinct handicap because he had never filled a full-time mission, and he was raised in a home lacking in gospel orthodoxy. These factors, coupled with his intense scientific and professional training, produced in him a seemingly aloof, detached, and, to an extent, cold quality in his earliest ministry in the stake. I heard one of my fellow high councilors say, a few weeks after President's Nelson's call, that the president's style was "as precise and antiseptic as an operating room."

But something changed a few months into his ministry. He began to exhibit a real depth of spirituality. He also began to show leadership ability, more so than any other man I had known in all my years of Church service. He was always a man of enormous talents and also one of the most buoyant and constantly optimistic men I have ever known. In his ministry he began to radiate goodness and ability and to inspire great confidence. However, outwardly his administrative acts continued to be characterized by the precision and deftness of a surgical operation. There was no fat in his meetings. They were all bone and muscle, with a heart beneath. He learned very quickly how to delegate. He was a great exemplar for the young people and inspired many to excel in their schooling and professions. Above all, he was dedicated to the

Lord and His Church. In any setting, he was never reluctant to proclaim his faith in God, and his allegiance to His Church and its leaders.

President Nelson's superior leadership ability was most evident in council meetings and from the pulpit. No one hearing him speak or listening to him pray could doubt his sincerity of heart or his great capacity.

In my diary for January 14, 1968, I commented on the astounding spiritual growth of the President and made the following prediction:

> Should this newly emerging spirituality become his dominant characteristic, it would not be unreasonable to predict that one day Russell M. Nelson will sit in the leading councils of the Church.

"AN EXAMPLE OF HOW THE LORD REVEALS DIVINE TRUTH"

One of the most profound spiritual experiences of my life occurred while serving as stake executive secretary in the Bonneville Stake under the leadership of President Russell M. Nelson. President Nelson liked holding meetings of the stake presidency very early on Sunday mornings. As I drove from our home to the stake center very early on Sunday, November 23, 1969, the thought suddenly came to me that a significant change would soon take place in my life. A few minutes later, I was sitting in the stake presidency meeting with Presidents Russell M. Nelson, Albert R. Bowen, and Joseph B. Wirthlin. In his first act of the day, President Nelson mentioned that he had been strongly impressed that they should replace our long-time bishop, Keith S. Smith of the Yalecrest Ward, at their coming Ward Conference in January or February of 1970. Presidents Bowen and Wirthlin concurred.

As the brethren discussed this change, the Spirit whispered to me that I would be designated as Bishop Smith's successor. So moved was I by this impression, that I recorded it in my church "Record" book, which I used to take notes as the stake executive secretary. That evening, when I returned home, I also recorded the impression in my personal diary.

I heard no further mention of a possible change in the Yalecrest Ward bishopric from that day forward. Many weeks passed. In January 1970 my wife, Helen, and I drove to Las Vegas, Nevada, where I attended a legal seminar over the span of several days. Helen and I returned to Salt Lake City on January 19, 1970.

At a small town near Cedar City, we stopped, and I called home to ask the children to get in touch with someone involved in my Church duties. Our daughter, Suzanne, answered the phone and gave me two messages: that President McKay had died and that President Russell M. Nelson wished to speak with me as soon as I returned. Helen and I discussed these two items on the way home, especially dwelling on the passing of the Prophet, David O. McKay, and of the possible changes this might bring about at Church headquarters. However, we could not see how this would impact us personally in any way. How little we knew.

As to the call from President Nelson, this was nothing unusual since we were in frequent contact about stake matters because of my call as stake executive secretary. So it was in this state of oblivion that we arrived home. I immediately called President Nelson, who said he wished to visit with me in our home. This touched off the memory of the revelation on my way to a meeting of the stake presidency and of President Nelson's comment about reorganizing the bishopric of the Yalecrest Ward. This prompted me to tell Helen she should not change into her nightclothes, as the President would wish to speak with her also.

When President Nelson arrived at our home soon after the telephone call, he was accompanied by his counselors, and the call was extended to me to serve as the bishop of the Yalecrest Ward. I then read to them the diary entry I had made following the meeting in December when it was revealed to me I was to become the bishop of this ward. To this President Nelson said, addressing his counselors, "See, I told you that Frank knew about this."

There is a touching personal postscript to this little incident involving my call as a bishop by President Nelson. In one of the final stake conferences President Nelson conducted as a stake president in 1971, we had Elder Ezra Taft Benson as a conference visitor. In a priesthood leadership session, Elder Benson admonished the brethren that they should pray for and rejoice in the success of their brethren, and particularly their leaders. Heeding this counsel, during the concluding general session of the conference, I prayed silently and fervently for President Nelson as he spoke. I recall that he was developing the theme of "Blessed are the Peacemakers," but in conclusion he paused for a lengthy period of time, and then told the saints that he wanted to share a personal spiritual experience. He referred to the spiritual manifestations that accompanied my call as a bishop of the Yalecrest Ward and related the experience from his perspective. He said that on Sunday, November 23, 1969, he received a clear impression that I should be called as a bishop. He then told the saints of the visit he made to my home with his counselors in January of 1970, of extending the call, and then having me read my own diary entry from November 23, in which I recorded my independent spiritual impression that I would be called. He testified of the reality of the gift of revelation, and he said that this was an example of how the Lord reveals divine truth to the hearts and minds of different people simultaneously.

Here is a final postscript to this experience: While serving as president of the Bonneville Stake, succeeding President Nelson, it was my privilege to call and ordain many bishops. On three separate occasions, after installing a new bishop in the stake, I was later approached by President Nelson, who told me that before being released as stake president, he had been impressed that these same brethren would one day be called as bishops. This occurred with numerous bishops that I called, including, as I recall, John Gaines, Keith Romney, and Joseph Fielding Smith, Jr. It was to me the clearest indication that President Nelson had the gift of prophecy in abundance.

"THE CHIEF ADVOCATE FOR RUSSELL M. NELSON WAS PRESIDENT LEE"

In 1971 President Russell M. Nelson was released as president of the Bonneville Stake in order to accept the calling from the First Presidency to serve as General President of the Sunday School.

I was in a truly unique position to observe this transition behind the scenes, because of my call in 1970 to serve as the secretary to the First Presidency. As fate would have it, I was also called to replace President Nelson as president of the Bonneville Stake.

The first discussions about calling a replacement for longtime General Sunday School Superintendent Lawrence McKay, a son of the late Prophet, occurred in the late spring of 1971. Coincidentally, it occurred at the same time that the Brethren were considering President Nelson's request to be absent from the stake for a lengthy period of time in order to attend a key medical meeting to be held in Moscow in the Soviet Union. There were several men being considered for this key calling, including President Nelson. It was evident to me that President Nelson was the first choice of the Brethren because he had strong administrative abilities, the ability to relate to the academic community, and a solid grounding in church doctrine. The chief advocate for Russell M. Nelson was President Harold B. Lee, then serving as first counselor in the First Presidency, and who in a few months would become President of the Church.

I have a very vivid recollection of the meeting of the First Presidency in which this discussion occurred, because of a private spiritual impression I received during the meeting. When the Brethren discussed the possibility of issuing this new call to Russell M. Nelson, I received a powerful inner whispering that I would be called to serve in the presidency of the Bonneville Stake.

Within a few days of this event, which probably occurred in late May or early June of 1971, President Russell M. Nelson was selected and then called as the General President of the Sunday School. President Nelson selected Joseph B. Wirthlin, his counselor in the Bonneville Stake Presidency, as his first Assistant, and Richard L. Warner, incumbent President of the University First Stake as his second Assistant. The decision was made that the new presidency would be announced at June Conference. This, of course, meant that a reorganization of both the Bonneville and University First Stakes.

Plans were immediately set to reorganize the presidency of the Bonneville Stake. I recall that President Harold B. Lee decided at the last minute to attend the stake conference where President Nelson was released. This he did, I am sure, as a sign of his personal esteem for President Nelson. President Lee presided at the meeting, although the official conference visitors were Elder Delbert L. Stapley of the Twelve and L. Brent Goates, a Regional Representative of the Twelve (a precursor calling to the present-day Area Seventy).

Elder Stapley and Brother Goates conducted the usual interviews, and in fulfillment of the strong impression I had received a few weeks earlier in a meeting of the First Presidency, I was called as stake president to succeed President Nelson.

There were thousands of people in attendance at the Sunday morning stake conference, the largest ever attendance at any stake conference in my memory. This was due to the great love and respect that the people had for President Nelson. They recognized, as did I, that this was a great man with a great future ahead of him.

The outgoing presidency, Russell M. Nelson, Albert R. Bowen, and Joseph B. Wirthlin spoke, as did I, my wife Helen, Sister Dantzel Nelson, L. Brent Goates, Elder Stapley, and President Lee. In his remarks, President Lee spoke in very glowing terms about President Nelson and his unique capabilities for service in the Kingdom. President Lee was also very generous in his support of me, expressing thanks for my services with the First Presidency. In retrospect, it is difficult to think of a more dramatic way in which President Lee could have strengthened our hand than in appearing the way he did.

"THEY HELD DANTZEL NELSON HOSTAGE"

While serving as president of the Bonneville Stake, President Nelson continued to pursue his extremely busy medical practice. He was on the cutting edge of open-heart surgery in both the United States and the world and had an impeccable worldwide reputation among his peers. Accordingly, he was frequently called upon to travel to speak to various medical gatherings. This continued after he became General President of the Sunday School.

A few weeks after his call to the Sunday School, in August of 1971, President Nelson attended a very prestigious Soviet medical conference held in Russia. This was during the Cold War, when it was very difficult to get in or out of the Soviet Union. The timing of this particular medical meeting coincided with the holding of the Church's first Area Conference, which was held in Manchester, England in 1971. In his capacity as General President of the Sunday School, President Nelson was also invited by the First Presidency to participate in the Area Conference. This posed a significant logistical problem for President Nelson, as his medical duties in Russia would conflict with the Area Conference in England. He concluded that he could go to Russia, begin the medical meetings there, then fly to England to be with the Brethren for the Area Conference, and then return to Russia to conclude his medical duties. When President Nelson went to the Soviet authorities, and explained his dilemma, they could not understand why he would want to leave Moscow to go to England for a religious meeting. They were very suspicious of his motives, and so for a long time withheld permission for him to leave. They finally relented and allowed him to go, but would not allow Dantzel Nelson, his wife, to accompany him. They insisted that she remain in Moscow until President Nelson returned. In effect, they held Dantzel Nelson hostage in the Soviet Union while President Nelson attended the first Area Conference in the history of the Church.

I should note one historic event that occurred during President Nelson's brief visit to England during this conference. On Friday evening, August 27, 1971, President Joseph Fielding Smith requested that his counselors and the General Authorities present for the

Area Conference convene in a special Council Meeting of the First Presidency and the Quorum of the Twelve held in the conference room of the Piccadilly Hotel in Manchester, England. Present at this meeting was Church President Joseph Fielding Smith; his first counselor, President Harold B. Lee; President Spencer W. Kimball, who was then President of the Quorum of the Twelve; and members of the Twelve, Marion G. Romney, Richard L. Evans, Howard W. Hunter, Gordon B. Hinckley, Thomas S. Monson, and Boyd K. Packer. With two members of the First Presidency and seven members of the Twelve in attendance, this was only the second council meeting with a "quorum" present ever held outside of the United States. The first was also held in Manchester, England, in 1840. Also present at this historic meeting were Assistants to the Twelve, Henry D. Taylor and Marion D. Hanks; members of the First Council of the Seventy, Paul H. Dunn and Loren C. Dunn; and Presiding Bishop, Victor L. Brown. Besides these General Authorities, there were present D. Arthur Haycock, W. Jay Eldredge, Russell M. Nelson, Joe J. Christensen, and myself.

It is significant to note that present at this meeting were six brethren who ultimately would serve as Presidents of the Church: Joseph Fielding Smith, Harold B. Lee, Spencer W. Kimball, Howard W. Hunter, Gordon B. Hinckley, and Thomas S. Monson. [Editor's note: President Nelson would be the seventh future President present in the meeting.]

It was a great privilege for me to also attend this historic meeting, and act as the scribe and secretary for the proceedings at the feet of Prophets, Seers, and Revelators.

"THE MOST TECHNICALLY PERFECT SURGERY HE HAD EVER PERFORMED"

President Russell M. Nelson had a special and unique relationship with President Spencer W. Kimball. He first met President Kimball in 1964, when he was called as president of the Bonneville Stake by President Kimball and Elder LeGrand Richards of the Twelve. In hindsight, we see the auspicious hand of the Lord in that first acquaintance, as a decade later President Nelson would save President Kimball's live in a delicate heart surgery, and two decades later he would fill the vacancy in the Twelve created by Elder Richards' death.

By the early 1970's, President Kimball, who was second in seniority in the Twelve behind President Harold B. Lee, was in extremely poor health. He was suffering from a wide array of physical maladies, the most serious of which were a recurring cancer in his throat and a heart condition. I recall that during the August 1971 Manchester Area Conference, President Kimball sought out the advice of President Nelson about his heart. I do not know the exact medical diagnosis beyond the fact that President Kimball was essentially suffering from congestive heart failure.

In April of 1972 President Kimball reached a crisis. He was dying and reached out to President Nelson for options. A special meeting of the First Presidency was called to discuss the grim prognosis with President Kimball. Invited to the meeting were Dr. Russell M. Nelson and Dr. Ernest L. Wilkinson. I was serving at the time as secretary to the First Presidency.

President Harold B. Lee asked the doctors about the risks to the life of President Kimball. President Nelson and Dr. Wilkinson were not overly optimistic about the prospects and rated the surgery as extremely risky.

I recall that President Kimball spoke up and told the First Presidency, "Brethren, I'm an old man and ready to die. Perhaps a younger, more vigorous man should be called to the Twelve to take my seat."

At that moment President Harold B. Lee pounded the desk with his fist and said, "Spencer! You are not to die!"

"Then," said President Kimball, "I will have the operation."

The operation was set, with President Nelson as the surgeon.

President Lee later told me that the night before the surgery, President Nelson came to President Lee and President Tanner and asked for a special blessing, which they gave to him.

The following day was the weekly meeting of the First Presidency and the Twelve in the Upper Room of the Temple. President Kimball's chair was empty, of course, as he was on the operating table at that time, and each man in the room was keenly aware of his absence. During the meeting, at which I acted as the scribe, I was quietly summoned out of the room to take a phone call. It was word that President Kimball's open-heart surgery was successful. I handed a message to President Lee in the Council Room, and he read it silently to himself, then reported it to the Brethren.

As President Lee read the message, I detected the first sign of emotion on his part. He said in a quavering voice, "The Lord has heard and answered our prayers!"

A day or two later, I spoke with President Nelson about the surgery. He told me, also with emotion in his voice, that it was the most technically perfect surgery he had ever performed as a surgeon!

"He 'Grounded' the Prophet"

During the 1970's and 1980's President Russell M. Nelson had a delightful doctor-patient relationship with many of the highest leaders of the Church.

In the early months of the administration of President Spencer W. Kimball, I had a long visit with President Russell M. Nelson while the two of us waited in line at a wedding reception. President Nelson told me that he had recently received an urgent call to go to the Prophet's home, where he found that his blood pressure was dangerously high. President Nelson told me that he "grounded" the Prophet for the weekend, and as his doctor, forbad him to keep any appointments or attend any meetings. He said that President Kimball unwillingly consented, and that the next Monday he visited the Prophet and found that the enforced rest had brought his blood pressure down to an acceptable level.

On another occasion, I was taking my seat on the stand at a stake meeting, and I heard an interchange between President Nelson and President Hugh B. Brown, former counselor in the First Presidency and a senior member of the Twelve. As the two of them shook hands, President Brown said to President Nelson, "Can you operate on me and restore my ego?" Without missing a beat, President Nelson replied, "According to my diagnosis, you don't suffer from any loss of ego!"

Speaking of President Brown, he was a great man, and a true original. As a member of the Garden Park Ward, he had known Russell M. Nelson since the latter was a small boy, living around the corner. At the time of the dedication of the Washington D.C. Temple in 1974, President Brown was very aged and most feeble, but he yearned to attend the dedication. Through the kindness of a very wealthy member of the Church, a private jet was placed at President Brown's disposal, so that he could travel in comfort. Accompanying him on his trip were some of his family members as companions, Dr. Truman Madsen of BYU as resident philosopher and raconteur, and President Russell M. Nelson as his private physician.

"THE CALL OF RUSSELL M. NELSON TO THE TWELVE WAS HISTORIC"

The call of Russell M. Nelson to the Twelve was historic. At that time, of course, President Kimball was in very poor health. He was suffering from the mounting debilities of old age and was largely confined to his apartment in the former Hotel Utah, now the Joseph Smith Memorial Building. At the time, in 1984, President Kimball's counselors were President Marion G. Romney and President Gordon B. Hinckley. President Romney was also not well, and was largely confined to his home in the Bonneville Stake.

President Hinckley was most wise during this crucial period, which had no precedent in the history of the Church. Never before or since has the First Presidency had only a single active counselor, save for a few months when the Prophet Joseph Smith was confined in the Liberty Jail. In any event, President Hinckley carried on the work with remarkable stability, wisdom, and aplomb.

President Hinckley and I would often visit President Kimball in his apartment, and we found that he was at his best following a good night's sleep. President Hinckley spoke confidentially to Brother D. Arthur Haycock, the Prophet's private secretary; the Church security man, who was always on duty at the Prophet's residence; and with Winnifred Eyring, his sister-in-law, who was often at the residence; and asked them to call when the Prophet was in his best form. On those occasions, I would go over to the Hotel with President Hinckley. So, the pattern for many months is that we would wait until word came through Brother Haycock that President Kimball was alert and up to a visit, and then President Hinckley and I would go over to appraise the Prophet on various issues facing the First Presidency.

During this same period, there had been two vacancies in the Quorum of the Twelve for many months. It was the sense of the other members of the Twelve that the vacancies ought to be filled, but President Hinckley was reluctant to move forward without the clear direction of the President of the Church.

One Thursday morning, we went, as before, to the President's home, having learned through Brother Haycock that President

Kimball was alert and cheerful and anxious to speak with his counselor, President Gordon B. Hinckley. It was a beautiful morning, and the apartment was fresh and clean and a sweet spirit pervaded the room. He was freshly shaven and sat in a chair at the dining room table. President Hinckley and I sat down at the table, and President Hinckley began briefing the Prophet on several matters. The final matter was posed by President Hinckley as a question: "What would you like to do about the vacancies in the Quorum of the Twelve?" President Kimball responded, "Why don't you poll the members of the Twelve and get their recommendations as to who they feel are worthy and able to become Apostles."

So President Gordon B. Hinckley did that, and the two names that were universally recommended were Russell M. Nelson and Dallin H. Oaks. A few days later, we were back at the Prophet's apartment, and President Hinckley presented the two names to the Prophet and said, "President, it is the sense of all of the Apostles that Brother Nelson and Brother Oaks be called to the Twelve." President Kimball considered this and then said in a strong voice, "That is right!"

A few days following the sustaining of the two new Apostles, I was present in the Upper Room of the Temple when President Nelson was ordained. (Elder Oaks' ordination was delayed a few weeks until he concluded some professional responsibilities). It was most moving to all of those present that President Spencer W. Kimball was there in person, as was his First Counselor, President Marion G. Romney. This placed a sweet divine imprimatur on the rightness of this call to the Apostleship!

"A DEEP SENSE OF HUMILITY"

From my observations, President Russell M. Nelson commenced his service in the Twelve with a deep sense of humility. By that time, I had been closely associated with him for nearly thirty years, but never before had I seen him take on the role of a student and learner quite like I observed in his early apostolic service. He quickly learned and mastered the procedures and organization of the vastly complex Church organization. He sought counsel. He listened very carefully. I believe that he was aware that his early experience in the Church was unusual, and he willingly sat at the feet of the senior Apostles who had been serving in most cases for decades and who had years of service as missionaries, bishops, and mission presidents behind them.

Two of President Nelson's greatest spiritual benefactors were President Harold B. Lee, who saw great promise in him, and President Spencer W. Kimball, who called him to the Twelve. In a way, President Nelson is an amalgam of the spiritual qualities of these two great men. President Lee was a visionary, an architect; and President Kimball was an indefatigable worker and one of the kindest human beings I have ever known. Both of these qualities of vision and kindness are possessed by President Nelson.

Because of his stature as a medical doctor, I believe that President Nelson enjoyed a respect and deference from the senior members of the Twelve and the First Presidency that was unusual. The same thing can be said for Elder Dallin H. Oaks, who was Chief Justice of the Utah Supreme Court. Not since the call of President J. Reuben Clark to the First Presidency by President Grant in 1933 has a man in the leading councils had such a powerful reputation outside the circle of the Church. But President Nelson did not presume any special status because of his worldly reputation. Rather, he assumed the role of a student and disciple.

One of the earliest decisions of President Hinckley with respect to the assignments to be given to President Nelson in his apostolic service was his special call to work to open the door to the preaching of the gospel in the former Soviet Union. President Nelson was a natural for this assignment. I recall President

Hinckley mentioning on more than one occasions the providential connection Brother Nelson had with Russia during his medical practice. He had traveled several times to Russia and learned the rudiments of the language. His preeminent medical reputation in the world, coupled with his innate interest in the lands of Russia and Eastern Europe, made him a perfect fit for this most important role. This role, of opening the doors of the Iron Curtain for the entry of the Lord's ministers, must surely stand as one of the greatest contributions by a member of the Twelve in the past century.

"PRESIDENT NELSON HAD SPECIAL RESPONSIBILITY FOR PATRIARCHS"

From 1986 through 1991, my interaction with President Nelson was limited, as during that time I was called to serve as a General Authority and resided much of that time in Brazil.

In 1994, three years after concluding my active service as a General Authority, I received a telephone call from President Russell M. Nelson, then a member of the Twelve. At the time I was serving as a stake patriarch, having been ordained in 1982, before my call as a General Authority. I went over to his office, and he said to me, "Brother Gibbons, the Brethren want you to serve as the patriarch at large for the Church." At the time, President Nelson had special responsibility for patriarchs. So, for sixteen years, from 1994 to 2010, I served in this special role under the direction of President Nelson. Whenever there was a member of the Church from an outlying area traveling to Salt Lake City and seeking a patriarchal blessing, the Twelve would always send them over to my apartment. That happened many, many times, and I gave hundreds of blessings to latter-day saints from some of the most remote corners of the world, including from China, Central Asia, Africa, and the former Soviet Union. I occasionally counseled with President Nelson about the blessings I was giving, and he gave me much counsel and encouragement. He was especially interested in the blessings given to those from China or the former Soviet Union, as he carried a special mandate to carry the gospel to those nations.

"THE SPECIAL KINDNESS OF PRESIDENT NELSON"

My final conversation with President Russell M. Nelson was in many ways the most touching to me personally. Following the death of my eternal companion, Helen Bay Gibbons, President Nelson attended her funeral. Before going to the chapel, President Nelson came to the Relief Society room, where Helen lay surrounded by members of the family. I was seated in an armchair beside my late wife. President Nelson came directly to my side, knelt down beside me, placed his hand on my shoulder, and spoke to me privately for five minutes or so. I was overwhelmed that one of the Lord's Apostles would show that level of kindness to me, even to the extent of kneeling to offer me comfort. He spoke to me of his love for me and my wife and family, of his long service in the Sunday School General Presidency with my wife as a member of his General Board, of our service together in high council and stake presidency callings in the Bonneville Stake, and of our years together serving in different but intersecting roles at Church headquarters.

During the funeral, President Nelson spoke at the conclusion of the program, reading a letter of condolence from the First Presidency. I was very interested to observe how intently he listened to all of the sermons, and especially to the musical numbers. Then, to my great surprise, President Nelson lingered following the services and positioned himself by the door, shaking hands with each and every one of my posterity—children, grandchildren, and great-grandchildren alike—and speaking words of comfort and encouragement to each of them.

In the weeks and months since this event, I have often pondered the special kindness of President Nelson on this occasion. It seems to be a sort of epitome of his long life of service. He is unfailingly kind. He is aware of people around him. He is always willing to put himself out in service to others and to go far beyond the extra mile.

Knowing and serving under this great Prophet, Seer, and Revelator has been one of the greatest blessings of my life!

LETTER FROM PRESIDENT RUSSELL M. NELSON TO THE FAMILY OF FRANCIS M. GIBBONS

July 18, 2016

Dearest family of Elder Francis M. Gibbons:

With the honorable graduation of your great father, it is appropriate to give thanks to our Heavenly Father for Frank's remarkable life of service. About 52 years ago, while I was serving as president of the Salt Lake Bonneville Stake, I called Francis M. Gibbons to be the stake executive secretary. Later, I was impressed to call him as Bishop of the Yalecrest Ward. In 1971, when I was released as stake president, the Lord called Francis M. Gibbons as the new stake president!

You know about his later faithful service as Secretary to the First Presidency of the Church, followed by five years as a General Authority Seventy. In that calling he carried a huge load, serving in the South America North, Brazil, and North America Southwest Area Presidencies.

Every assignment he filled with dignity and distinction. His enduring assignment as Stake Patriarch became the capstone of his life of consecrated service.

Surely his most notable work was in his family with your dear mother, Helen. They are justifiably proud of their children, Suzanne, Mark, Ruth and Daniel. Each of you has added luster to this great family with your own children and grandchildren.

At this tender time of separation, we are all comforted and sustained by the knowledge that life is eternal. Your great father will be reunited with your dear mother. They will be resurrected, glorified, and exalted, with every blessing that God bestows upon His faithful children. What noble examples for all to follow!

Please know of my enduring love for your dear parents, and of my gratitude for each of their remarkable posterity. My love is with you always.

With everlasting affection,

Russell M. Nelson

ABOUT THE AUTHOR

During his ninety-five-years of life, Francis M. Gibbons (1921-2016) was a student, a newspaper carrier, a grocer, a bookkeeper, a certified court reporter, a missionary, a sailor, a laborer, a university and law student, a trial lawyer, a church leader, and a prolific writer of more than thirty books. A lifelong member of The Church of Jesus Christ of Latter-day Saints, he served as a bishop, stake president, stake patriarch, and as the secretary to the First Presidency under four Presidents of the

Church. For more than thirty years until his death at the age of 95, he was also a General Authority or *Emeritus* General Authority of the Church. In the autumn of his life, from 1994 to 2010, he also served as patriarch at large to the Church. He was married for seventy years to Helen Bay Gibbons, who preceded him in death in 2015. They had four children and eighteen grandchildren.

*For more information about books
by Francis M. Gibbons:*

amazon.com/author/francismgibbons

ABOUT THE EDITOR

Daniel Bay Gibbons is a writer, publisher and practicing attorney living in Holladay, Utah. The youngest son of Francis M. Gibbons and Helen Bay Gibbons, he is a former trial attorney and judge and is the author of more than sixteen books, including *Nethermost: Missionary Miracles in Lowly Places*, and the historical novel *Last Ride To Carthage*. He has served as a full-time missionary, as a temple ordinance worker, twice as a bishop, and as president of the Russia Novosibirsk Mission. He currently serves as a ward Young Men President and as a Clearance Analyst in the Church's Missionary Department.

He is married to Julie Glenn Gibbons, and they have five children and eight grandchildren.

*For more information about books
by Daniel Bay Gibbons:*

amazon.com/author/danielbaygibbons

INDEX

91045707R00070

Made in the USA
Columbia, SC
11 March 2018